THE JUSTICE METHOD

RUSTY BRATZLER

The Official Workbook Used by **JUSTICE TUMBLING CO.**

The Justice Method (U) ISBN_____ Copyright © 2019 by Clay Clark Publishing 1100 Suite #100 Riverwalk Terrace Jenks, OK 74037. Most often, printed in the United States of America. All rights reserved. No part of this book may be used reproduced in any manner whatsoever without written permission of Rusty Bratzler. For additional information, address Clay Clark Publishing, 1100 Riverwalk Terrace #1100, Jenks, OK, 74037. Clay Clark publishing books may be purchased for educational, business or sales promotional use. Additional FUN FACT: The average human head weighs 10 to 11 pounds. For more information about ordering additional copies of this book email: info@ThriveTimeShow.com. For a good time visit ThriveTimeShow.com.

SPECIAL FOREWORD BY CLAY CLARK.

I host an iTunes chart-topping podcast (www.ThrivetimeShow.com) and I grow businesses for a living and I've been honored to mentor Rusty in the game of business for the past year. However, as a father I have had the opportunity to pay Rusty Bratzler to help my kids to improve in their tumbling skills. As the father of 4 girls, both my wife and I have been amazed with the improvement that the girls have shown over the past 3 years. Their improvement, as a result of his coaching, has been nothing short of amazing.

On a business level, Rusty has been a business coaching client of mine for over a year and it has been an honor to watch him diligently implement the proven business path with the same intensity, drive and focus with which he coaches our daughters.

> "A friendship founded on business is better than a business founded on friendship."
> **- John D. Rockefeller**
> (American Businessman and Philanthropist)

Despite having been a startup business just one short year ago, Rusty is a veteran in the world of tumbling. As the host of The Thrivetime Show Podcast, I've had the opportunity to personally interview America's business leaders, countless millionaires and billionaires who all achieved tremendous success in part because, much like Rusty, they chose to NEVER lose their passion for their PURPOSE. As far as I'm concerned, Rusty is at the top 1% of his profession just like many of my past ThrivetimeShow.com guests including:

Michael Levine - The public relations consultant of choice for Nike, Prince, Michael Jackson, President Clinton and Charlton Heston

Wolfgang Puck - The man whose name has become synonymous with fine dining, Horst Schultz, the co-founder of Ritz-Carlton

David Robinson - The NBA Hall of Fame basketball player, turned successful investor and entrepreneur.

Scott Belsky - The founder of Behance and the Chief Product Officer and Executive Vice President of Adobe.

John Maxwell - The 8x New York Times Best-Selling Author and Leadership Expert.

Guy Kawasaki - The legendary Former Key Apple Employee Turned Venture Capitalist and Best Selling Author.

Sharon Lechter - The New York Times Best-Selling Co-Author of Rich Dad Poor Dad.

Pastor Craig Groeschel - The Senior pastor of the largest church in America with over 100,000 weekly attendees (Lifechurch.tv).

David Bach - One of America's most trusted financial experts and has written nine consecutive New York Times bestsellers with 7 million+ books in print.

Zack O'Malley Greenburg - The Senior Editor for Forbes and 3x Best-Selling Author.

John Lee Dumas - The Most Downloaded Business Podcaster of All-Time (EOFire.com),

Seth Godin - New York Times Best-Selling Author of Purple Cow, and former Yahoo! Vice President of Marketing,

Dan Heath - New York Times Best-Selling Author of Made to Stick and Duke University Professor

Lee Cockerell - The former Executive Vice President of Walt Disney World who once managed 40,000 employees.

Ben Shapiro - Conservative Talk Pundit, Frequent Fox News Contributor, Political Commentator and Best-Selling Author,

See additional guests at Thrivetimeshow.com

If you are entrusting your kids to the coaching and training that Justice Tumbling provides you are in GREAT HANDS.

> "If you are entrusting your kids to the coaching and training that Justice Tumbling provides you are in GREAT HANDS."
> **- Clay Clark**
>
> Co-host with Dr. Robert Zoellner of the ThriveTime Radio Show, Founder of DJConnection.com, EITRLounge.com, EpicPhotos.com, MakeYourLifeEpic.com, Thrive15.com (As seen on Forbes, Bloomberg, YahooFinance, Fast Company, etc.), U.S. SBA Entrepreneur of the Year, Some People Don't Need A Hype Man...I Do (WATCH), Contributor for Entrepreneur Magazine, What is Thrive15.com? U.S. Chamber National Quality Award Winner, Co-Founder of 5 Kids (Read Fast Company Article for Proof), Speaker of Choice For many of America's largest and smallest companies.

"MY DAUGHTER DID COMPETITIVE POWER TUMBLING FOR 7 YEARS AT ANOTHER GYM. SHE LOST HER DRIVE, COMPETITIVE SPIRIT, AND MOST OF ALL HER SMILE DUE TO THE LACK OF 1 ON 1 COACHING. SHE FELT LIKE ROBOT JUST BEING PUT THROUGH THE MOTIONS. SHE DECIDED TO QUIT TO PURSUE SCHOOL CHEER AND COMPETITIVE CHEER. HER VERY FIRST DAY AT JUSTICE SHE COULD NOT STOP SMILING AND HAVING A GREAT TIME LEARNING FROM THESE GREAT COACHES. JUSTICE IS ALL SHE TALKS ABOUT. SO THAT BEING SAID THANK YOU JUSTICE TUMBLING FOR GIVING MY DAUGHTER A REASON TO SMILE AGAIN AND HAVE FUN."

— **CHRISTOPHER PRIDEAUX**

TUMBLING 101

"EACH ONE OF US HAS A FIRE IN OUR HEART FOR SOMETHING. IT'S OUR GOAL IN LIFE TO FIND IT AND KEEP IT LIT."

- MARY LOU RETTON
Olympic Gold Medal Winning Gymnast

Chapter 1. Who is Justice?	10
Chapter 2. A Message to Parents	12
Chapter 3. Owners Bios	14
Chapter 4. Intro / How to use Workbook	17
Chapter 5. Disclaimer	18
Chapter 6. Road Map	20
Chapter 7. Justice Tumbling Progressions	23
Chapter 8. Commonly Used Terms & Bad Words	27
Chapter 9. Mental Blocks	31
Chapter 10. Tiny Tumbling	35
Chapter 11. Beginner Tumbling	41
Chapter 12. Novice Tumbling	47
Chapter 13. Intermediate Tumbling	53
Chapter 14. Advanced Tumbling	59
Chapter 15. Elite Tumbling	65
Chapter 16. Stunt	71

"IF YOU OR YOUR ATHLETES ARE LOOKING FOR A SAFE, FUN, AND QUALITY TUMBLING EXPERIENCE, THEN JUSTICE TUMBLING IS YOUR NEW HOME. THE FAMILY OWNED BUSINESS PROVIDES EXCELLENT CUSTOMER SERVICE, KNOWLEDGEABLE INSTRUCTORS, AND CREATES A POSITIVE/SUPPORTIVE ENVIRONMENT FOR STUDENTS TO LEARN. THE OWNERS METHODICALLY HAVE STRUCTURED THE CURRICULUM TO CONNECT WITH ALL LEARNING STYLES. VISUAL, AUDITORY, AND KINESTHETIC DRILLS WILL HAVE YOUR STUDENTS ACCOMPLISHING GOALS AND MASTERING SKILLS IN NO TIME. MAKE SURE TO ASK ABOUT THE JUSTICE PROGRAM PACKET FOR FURTHER INFORMATION."

- AUSTIN ROWES

WHO IS JUSTICE?

Justice Tumbling Company was founded by Rusty and Caitlin Bratzler. Our goal for Justice was to change the tumbling industry and provide a technique driven curriculum that not only gets results but keeps athletes safe. That's why this book was written. Justice Tumbling Company was not created for a particular type of athlete, but for all athletes who have a desire to tumble. Whether you're an all-star or high school cheerleader, gymnast, or just want to have a hobby that will blow people's minds, we'll get you started on the right path.

At Justice Tumbling Company, we're not just a gym, we're a family. From our friendly staff and cozy lounge, to our top of the line equipment and training techniques, you'll feel welcome as soon as you walk through the door. Our stress free atmosphere provides the perfect learning environment for athletes to be able to focus on their own skills while gaining self-confidence. We know that tumbling is more than just a physical sport, it's a mental mountain that every athlete must conquer within themselves. We use the drills and techniques that will prepare your athlete at the appropriate pace so that they have the confidence needed to achieve new skills. We started Justice Tumbling Company because we've personally seen recreational tumbling classes getting neglected and pushed aside. We've personally seen proper technique ignored, which puts athletes at risk of injury. We've seen mental blocks ruin an athletes career from skills being pushed too quickly. We've seen injustice in the world tumbling and we stand against it.

"JUSTICE TUMBLING, IT'S OWNERS, AND TEAM ARE ABSOLUTELY AMAZING! THE STUDENTS ARE TAUGHT THE PROPER TECHNIQUE OF TUMBLING, WHICH IS SO IMPORTANT! WE WERE INTRODUCED TO JUSTICE TUMBLING THROUGH SCHOOL CHEER, AND I CAN SAY WITH HONESTY, THAT AS LONG AS MY DAUGHTER IS INVOLVED WITH CHEER, SHE WILL NEVER TUMBLE ANYWHERE ELSE. THERE'S NO PLACE BETTER. RUSTY AND HIS TEAM OF COACHES GET TO KNOW EVERY ATHLETE, AND MEETS THEM WHERE THEY ARE AT. OUR ONLY REGRET IS NOT HAVING MET RUSTY BEFORE NOW! SERIOUSLY, LOVE THE WAY THAT HE AND HIS STAFF ENCOURAGE AND BELIEVE IN HER ABILITY! CHOOSE JUSTICE. IT'LL MAKE A · WORLD OF DIFFERENCE IN YOUR ATHLETES OVERALL SKILL AND ABILITY"

— **VERONICA HIX**

A MESSAGE TO PARENTS

Hey Moms and Dads! We cannot begin to thank you enough for allowing us to be a part of your child's growth as an athlete. You've made the wise decision to join the Justice Tumbling Family along with the other countless parents who have witnessed the growth and success in their own child. Overtime, you too will see the Justice difference as your athlete begins to gain new skills, along with a new found confidence that will carry them to success even into adulthood. At Justice Tumbling Co., we know that this generation of athletes not only needs responsible adult coaches, but responsible adult mentors as well. In a world filled with so much hate, negativity, nastiness, and downright evil, parents need to know that the people who will be surrounding their children are of the highest quality. That they are held to the highest standard possible.

No one knows your child better than you do. With that being said, we invite you to join us on this journey. Through the ups and downs, your child will need your support, encouragement, and love to help them become the incredible human being they are meant to be. Read through this workbook with them, hold them accountable to their homework, and consistently let them know that you believe in them to achieve their goals. They need to know those things and they need to hear them from you. Listen to your athlete and tell them how proud of them you are for every single one of their new achievements.

Sometimes though, athletes need a little bit of space, and the pressures of having eyes on them may be less helpful and more stressful. When those times come, please feel free to use our comfortable lounges where the cameras around the gym allow you to see them perform without the added pressure. We truly value communication between coach, parent, and athlete and you may always come to us with any concerns you may have.

Again, welcome to the Justice Tumbling Family. We are so happy you've joined us and we promise you, you will not be disappointed!

Love,

Justice Tumbling Co.

"JUSTICE TUMBLING COMPANY HAS BEEN SO HELPFUL TO MY DAUGHTER. THEY DO SUCH A GREAT JOB OF MAKING THEIR ATHLETES FEEL COMFORTABLE AND CONFIDENT. EVERYONE IS FRIENDLY AND ENCOURAGING FROM THE TIME YOU WALK IN THE DOOR UNTIL THE TIME YOU EXIT. MY DAUGHTER LOVES THAT RUSTY ALWAYS GIVES HER FEEDBACK AFTER EACH TURN TO HELP HER
IMPROVE."

— MELISSA MCBROOM

MEET THE OWNERS

RUSTY BRATZLER

Hello my name is Rusty Bratzler and I am the owner of Justice Tumbling Company. Here at Justice we want everyone to feel at home so I wanted to give a quick background on me and how Justice Tumbling Company came to be. I have one older brother named Dusty who growing up played every sport you could think of. I tried most of those sports with him and could never find a sport that I was good at or enjoyed. My parents were always trying to find something for me to do that I was passionate about. At 9 years old I got into gymnastics and I loved it. My favorite part of gymnastics was floor because of the tumbling. Even in gymnastics, I wouldn't say tumbling became my passion. It wasn't until I quit gymnastics that my tumbling career actually started. After five years I was done with gymnastics but I still wanted to keep up my tumbling so I started classes at a competitive cheerleading gym called Cheers To You. Shannon Young was the allstar director of CTY at the time and came to one of my tumbling classes and asked if I would be interested in cheering. This was around my freshman year when I joined Bixby cheerleading with a few of my friends. One of my friends lost a bet and had to cheer for a year so I joined with him. We both ended up loving it and cheering for all four years of high school. The head coach of Bixby at the time was Stephanie Blackwell.

In those four years of high school Stephanie Blackwell and Shannon Young pushed me to be the best athlete I could be no matter what and I wouldn't be where I am today if it wasn't for them. They always pushed me when it came to my tumbling. Tumbling didn't come naturally to me. I was one of those athletes who had to put a lot of training in for every skill I got. I was always in the gym with my friends pushing for new skills and if I couldn't make it to the gym I was out in my yard practicing. My junior year of high school I broke my neck doing a triple front flip on a tumble track trying to impress a girl. Before a practice I was tumbling with my friends I had done the skill successfully multiple times. After a long three hour practice I decided to try it again to show off and did a two and a half front flip to my head. After breaking my C6 and C7 vertebrae I was blessed to be able to walk let alone tumble again. I remember the recovery process being terrible because I had to sit out and watch everyone else tumble. I didn't realize how much I actually enjoyed tumbling until I wasn't able to do it anymore. When I was released to tumble again I didn't deal with any kind of "block" because after sitting out and wanting to tumble for so long my "want" to tumble out weighed any fear I had. I was able to come back and finish out my senior year on varsity and my competitive cheer team Cheer Dynamix. After winning state and NCA twice in my high school cheer career I thought I was finished with cheer because I never planned on going to college. Shannon Young and Stephanie Blackwell convinced me that I had practiced too hard for my skills to not cheer at least one year in college. I attended the University of Central Oklahoma for one year where I met my beautiful wife and after cheering one year in college I knew school wasn't for me. I worked a lot of different jobs to support me and Caitlin through the years until I got into coaching. I never even considered coaching tumbling as an option and now after almost 10 years I couldn't imagine doing anything else. Tumbling was my first love and still is my passion. My favorite thing as a coach is to see kids find their passion in tumbling. I train my athletes the way I do in hopes that they never have to go through the injuries and falls I did growing up.

CAITLIN BRATZLER

Hi! I'm Caitlin Bratzler, and I am the other half owner of Justice Tumbling Co! We are so excited to welcome you to our second home, and I wanted to introduce myself and tell you a little bit about me. Family is something I am passionate about, and that is one reason why we started Justice Tumbling Co. We wanted a business where we could spend time together, while also making a difference in the lives of athletes of the cheer world. Let's be honest, if you know Rusty, then you know he spends about 90% of his time in the gym, so being able to be a part of Justice is great, because not only do I get to do this with Rusty, I also get to know all you parents and watch athletes thrive doing something they love. My role at Justice is working the front desk and taking care of all the enrollment and financial aspects of the gym. Other than running a business, I am a mom to my curly head son, Daxton, a dog mom to 3 crazy pups, and an Esthetician and Makeup Artist.

"LOVE IT HERE! BE READY TO WORK! IF YOU WANT TO GET KEEP YOUR TUMBLING SKILLS IN CHECK OR LEARN NEW ONES, ALL OF THE COACHES THERE WILL PUSH YOU. RUSTY IS A TUMBLING GURU TO SAY THE LEAST. HE WILL, WITHOUT A DOUBT, GIVE YO U
THE TOOLS TO BE SUCCESSFUL. ON SATURDAY'S THEY HAVE STUNTING CLASSES FOR BOTH GROUP AND PARTNER. SPENCER IS THE MAIN COACH. WITH HIM, IT MAY TAKE LONGER TO START WORKING HARDER SKILL BUT THAT'S ONLY BECAUSE HE MAKES SURE YOU HAVE PROPER TECHNIQUE BEFORE MOVING ON."

— **ALEX SEGOVIA**

INTRODUCTION

Welcome to The Justice Method.

Whether you're just starting on your tumbling journey, or you're a seasoned elite athlete, the proven techniques and processes found in this workbook are guaranteed to give you the tools needed to expand your abilities, knowledge, and confidence. We are so excited to see you grow into the UNBEATABLE athlete that we know you will become!

HOW TO USE THIS WORKBOOK

First step to using this workbook is to have the athlete fill out the roadmap on the following page no matter what level the athlete is. The roadmap will tell our coaching staff exactly WHY you are wanting to learn to tumble. After the why section of the roadmap page is to set realistic goals for three months, six months, and one year. Once goals are set its up to the athlete to determine how many hours a week they are willing to work IN THE GYM and AT HOME to accomplish those goals. The next step in the roadmap page is for athletes to rate themselves on a scale of one through ten on their FEARLESSNESS, DETERMINATION, AND COACHABILITY. The last step is to go to the progressions sheet in the workbook and check off which skills the athlete has MASTERED. That will help determine which level class the athlete should be in. Each level is broken up into three months. If the athlete is following the training in the class, doing the homework at home, and using the workbook there is no reason a athlete should get stuck in one class for more than three months. There is a notes section at the end of each level for the athlete to keep track of their tumbling career and make note of really good tumbling days and the rough tumbling days.

DISCLAIMER

 Justice Tumbling Company wants to help every athlete that walks through our door, but realistically we can't please everyone. We know every athlete is different and learns at their own pace but our coaches are here to provide the best tumbling technique no matter why the athlete is learning to tumble. Our coaches treat and train the children like athletes because we strongly believe cheerleading/tumbling is a sport. Unfortunately, a lot of the time, our jobs as coaches end up being just fixing bad habits instead...

 Every class, no matter the level will have drills set up to keep the athletes moving and shaping their skills even when they aren't working one on one with the coach. After stretching and warming up there is thirty minutes of intense tumbling. We expect tumbling to be a work out so for that thirty minutes the athletes should be constantly moving. The last ten to fifteen minutes of class focuses on conditioning whatever muscles that level of athlete needs for the skills they are working.

"EVEN WITH MY WHOLE TEAM THEY MADE SURE TO PAY VERY CLOSE DETAIL WITH EACH AND EVERY PERSON AND HELPED EVERYONE INDIVIDUALLY. THEY MADE EVERY PERSON FEEL IMPORTANT AND REALLY HELPED ME!"

- **JENNIFER TYLER**

"FROM A CHEERLEADERS POINT OF VIEW I'VE LEARNED MORE IN THE SHORT TIME I'VE BEEN AT THIS GYM THEN I'VE EVER GOTTEN IN AN ALL STAR ATMOSPHERE. THE COACHES TRULY CARE ABOUT YOU AND THE PROGRESS YOU MAKE! 10/10 RECOMMENDATION"

- **MAISE BURKE**

WHY?
WHY ARE YOU WANTING TO LEARN TO TUMBLE?
School Cheer?
All-Star Cheer?
Gymnastics?
Just for Fun?

GOALS
WHERE DO YOU WANT TO BE?
3 Months
6 Months
1 Year

Number of hours willing to work in the gym per week

Number of hours willing to work at home per week

ON A SCALE OF 1 TO 10
FEARLESSNESS
DETERMINATION
COACHABILITY

THE REWARD
NEW SKILLS
CONFIDENCE
GRATIFICATION
SUCCESS

BEGIN WITH THE END IN MIND. 21

WHY? _____

_____

_____

GOALS

3 MONTHS _____

6 MONTHS _____

1 YEAR _____

NUMBER OF HOURS WILLING TO WORK IN THE GYM PER WEEK? _____

NUMBER OF HOURS WILLING TO WORK AT HOME PER WEEK? _____

"You Cannot Conquer what you aren't commited to."
T.D. Jakes

New York Times
(Best-Selling Author &
Pastor of Potter's House Church)

"EXCELLENT TUMBLING GYM. EACH COACH DOES A GREAT JOB OF EXPLAINING TECHNIQUE, OFFERING CRITIQUE AND HELPING TUMBLERS IMPROVE THEIR SKILLS. THEY ALSO SHOW THE TUMBLERS HOW TO PERFORM EACH SKILL AND PROVIDE PLENTY OF DRILLS TO PERFECT THE SKILL.."

- JENNIFER LOVELAND

JUSTICE TUMBLING PROGRESSIONS

Think of a list of every tumbling skill there is and arrange them in an order that they SHOULD be learned. That's what progressions are. In the following pages are a list of running and standing tumbling progressions that ALL Justice Tumbling Coaches follow. Following progressions lead to confident skill building and consistency. Athletes who skip skills will always hit some sort of wall weather that is mental or physical. All the skills in the progression sheets are color coded by skill level. Our coaches never have the intention of holding your child back so if the coaches are continuing to work certain skills instead of moving on it is because the technique is not up to par to move on. There is a big difference in throwing a skill and throwing a skill correctly. Trust the process and follow these Justice Tumbling Company progressions and you will see results. Results don't always mean new skills. Sometimes cleaning up an old skill is just as important as learning a new skill. If parents or athletes have any questions about why they are working certain skills please feel free to ask!

RUNNING TUMBLING PROGRESSION SHEET

BEGINNER

- ☐ Lunge
- ☐ Handstand
  (step down)
- ☐ Cartwheel
  (into lunge and step in rebound)
- ☐ Round Off
  (power hurdle, two step, and running)

NOVICE

- ☐ Front Walkover
- ☐ Round Off Back Handspring
- ☐ Round Off Back Handspring Series
- ☐ Front Walkover Round Off Back Handspring

INTERMEDIATE

- ☐ Round Off Back Handspring Tuck (Round Off Tuck)
- ☐ Front Walkover Round Off Back Handspring Tuck
- ☐ Punch Front

ADVANCED

- ☐ Round Off Back Handspring Layout
- ☐ Round Off Whip
  (Round Off Back Handspring Whip)
- ☐ Punch Front Round Off Back Handspring Layout
- ☐ Round Off Whip Two Back Handsprings Layout

ELITE

- ☐ Round Off Back Handspring Full
- ☐ Round Off Arabian
  (Round Off Back Handspring Arabian)
- ☐ Specialty Through to a Full
  (Punch Front, Whip, or Arabian)
- ☐ Round Off Back Handspring Double Full
- ☐ Specialty Through to a Double Full
  (Punch Front, Whip, Arabian)

HOW MANY CAN YOU CHECK OFF?

STANDING TUMBLING PROGRESSION SHEET

BEGINNER
- ☐ Forward Roll
- ☐ Backward Roll
- ☐ Bridge (Bridge Kickover)
- ☐ Toe Touch

NOVICE
- ☐ Back Walkover
- ☐ Backward Extension Roll
- ☐ Back Handspring
- ☐ Toe Touch Back Handspring
- ☐ Series Back Handspring

INTERMEDIATE
- ☐ Three Back Handspring to Tuck
- ☐ Two Back Handspring to Tuck
- ☐ One Back Handspring Tuck
- ☐ Cartwheel Tuck
- ☐ Standing Tuck
- ☐ Toe Touch Tuck

ADVANCED
- ☐ Three Back Handsprings to Layout
- ☐ Two Back Handsprings to Layout
- ☐ One Back Handspring Layout

ELITE
- ☐ Three Back Handsprings to Full
- ☐ Two Back Handsprings to Full
- ☐ One Back Handspring to Full
- ☐ Cartwheel Full
- ☐ Standing full
- ☐ Toe Touch Full
- ☐ Three Back Handsprings to Double Full

HOW MANY CAN YOU CHECK OFF?

"WE'VE JUST TRANSITIONED OUT OF THE POWER TUMBLING WORLD INTO CHEER TUMBLING AND RUSTY HAS MADE IT SO DOABLE! HE DOESN'T JUST GIVE INSTRUCTIONS, HE DEMONSTRATES, USES DRILLS AND GIVES SPECIFIC DETAILED WAYS TO CORRECT SOMETHING. RUSTY IS ALWAYS RESPECTFUL OF THE TIME, AND THEY WASTE NONE! THAT HOUR IS PACKED AND SHE ALWAYS LEAVES IMPROVED!"

— **JAMIE HARRELL**

"WE LOVE THE ATMOSPHERE, PROFESSIONALISM AND KNOWLEDGE OF THE JUSTICE STAFF. MY DAUGHTER HAS PROGRESSED WITH SO MANY OF HER PERSONAL TUMBLING GOALS. RUSTY IS AMAZING AND PUSHES MY DAUGHTER TO HER FULL POTENTIAL. THANK YOU JUSTICE TUMBLING!!!"

— **TENLEY JIMISON**

COMMONLY USED TERMS AT JUSTICE

Consistent

Definition- Acting or done in the same way over time, especially so as to be fair or accurate. Unchanging in nature, standard, or effect over time.

Justice- When our coaches are looking at an athletes skill, we are looking to see if the skills and the technique in the skills are CONSISTENT. Consistency breeds confidence, therefore making moving on to new skills or learning new skills comes more naturally.

Master

Definition- Having or showing very great skill or proficiency. acquire complete knowledge or skill in (an accomplishment, technique, or art). To gain control of; overcome.

Justice- At Justice you will hear our coaches talk about MASTERED skills. Mastered skills are skills that the technique is up to par and skills that never have to be spotted. Eventually with enough practice and training all skills should be mastered skills.

Determination

Definition- Firmness of purpose; resoluteness. The process of establishing something exactly by calculation or research.

Justice- All our coaches at Justice love when an athlete comes in determined to get a new skill or clean up a new skill. Athletes always say they want a certain skill but are rarely determined enough to do all the training, conditioning and homework required.

Pressure

Definition- Continuous physical force exerted on or against an object by something in contact with it. The use of persuasion, influence, or intimidation to make someone do something.

Justice- When learning a skill there is always that moment when it is time for the coaches to move away and let the athlete do the skill on their own. The coaches continuing to "just stand there" or spotting a skill that doesn't need to be spotted can end up hurting the kid more than helping them. The goal of every skill is to be thrown without the coach's assistance. At the end of class, we like to do a "show and tell to put some PRESSURE on kids to motivate them to throw it on their own.

Fearlessness

Definition- Not the absence of fear, but the ability to overcome it in order to reach goals.

Justice- FEARLESSNESS is something that some athletes naturally have and something some athletes must train over time. Fearless athletes tend to learn skills at a faster pace because they can try skills without a coach, and without overthinking the skill.

Coachability

Definition- Capable of being easily taught and trained to do something better. Being able to take necessary criticism or pressure from a coach while keeping a positive attitude.

Justice- Some athletes when told to make a correction can do so the first try. Other athletes must be told the same correction multiple times or sometimes hundreds of times drawing out learning process. Coachable athletes when asked to try something new in a skill or a drill they do so with no questions asked making the learning process quick and enjoyable.

Alpha Athlete

Definition-

Alpha - Denoting a person who has a dominant role or position within a particular sphere.

Athlete- A person who is proficient in sports and other forms of physical exercise.

Justice- Alpha Athletes are athletes who take ALL of our coaches training and instruction. These are athletes who follow our progressions and take the time to master skills instead of rushing to the next skill. These athletes also try every drill our coaches throw at them with no complaints as well as do the homework given to them by their coaches. They are always asking questions about their skills and asking if there is something more they can be doing at home to progress their training. Most importantly these athletes always come in with a smile on their face like they want to be in the gym.

JUSTICE TUMBLING "BAD WORDS"

There are a few terms that are considered cuss words at Justice Tumbling Company. These words are CAN'T and MENTAL BLOCK. Both words have such a negative effect on the athlete's frame of mind that it makes learning skills or even tumbling all together very unenjoyable. If an athlete is telling themselves they CAN'T do something, whether it's a skill or drill, they are setting themselves up for failure or potentially getting hurt. Usually even if an athlete has the muscle and technique required for a skill, them telling themselves they CAN'T causes the athlete to doubt themselves and not perform the skill, drill, or pass the way they normally would. MENTAL BLOCKS are the same way. We at Justice Tumbling Company know that there are cases where kids really do struggle with blocks, but lately MENTAL BLOCK is a term that gets thrown around all the time when that's simply not the case. Justice Tumbling Company wants to develop a culture of confident tumbling to where these words are a thing of the past.

"RUSTY IS VERY HELPFUL, KNOWLEDGEABLE, FRIENDLY AND GOOD AT WHAT HE DOES. I RECOMMEND ANYONE WHO WANTS TO IMPROVE THEIR TUMBLING SKILLS COME SEE RUSTY AT JUSTICE TUMBLING CO. MY GIRLS HAVE MADE SIGNIFICANT IMPROVEMENTS IN JUST A FEW PRIVATE LESSONS. HE'S THE BEST AT WHAT HE DOES. I HIGHLY RECOMMEND HIM."

- **MILLIE GARCIA**

MENTAL BLOCKS

INTRO

What are mental blocks? A mental block is defined as an inability to recall some specific thing or perform some mental action. There are a lot of opinions on mental blocks when it comes to tumbling but just like every athlete is different, every "mental block" is different in its own way. In this chapter I am going to go over Justice Tumbling Company thoughts on mental blocks and how we deal with them. As I explained earlier in the book saying "mental block" in the gym is considered a curse word or bad word because I have seen it spread as a sickness through a team or program. Some of those
athletes may deal with a serious block but a majority of athletes either don't understand the technique of a skill, or they are not conditioned enough for the skill they are attempting to throw. Being afraid of a skill or having fear when attempting a skill is normal and is NOT a mental block. Every skill requires a certain amount of technique, conditioning, and mental toughness. At Justice Tumbling Company we push our athletes to consistently work on all three. Here are some things I have seen in my coaching career that lead to mental blocks in cheerleading/tumbling.

Falling- Probably the most obvious one. This can be the athlete taking a major fall during tumbling or the athlete witnessing a major fall. Unfortunately falling is a part of tumbling. Every athlete has taken a fall or will take a fall. It's just part of the sport. Training technique, mastering skills, and conditioning your body is the easiest was to prevent and lower your chances of taking a fall.

Performance Anxiety- Performance anxiety often gets mistaken for a tumbling block but is very different. Performance anxiety is defined as extreme nervousness experienced before or during participation in an activity taking place in front of an audience. These athletes tend to "block" during competition or tryouts. I have seen athletes block on a skill at practice, classes, and privates but when it comes to tryouts or
competition they have been able to throw their skill. These kinds of athletes need to remember that tumbling is supposed to be fun and not a job or something to stress about.

Growth Spurts- Athletes who gain skills at a young age and then have a growth spurt can find themselves struggling with a block because their bodies and skills feel different. Cheerleaders tend to learn their basics at a young age and then rarely work on
them. We train our athletes to understand that as they grow their skills must grow with them. That way when our athletes do have a growth spurt it is something we have prepared them for so it should not slow down their tumbling learning progress.

Fear of Failure- Tumbling is unnatural for the body and learning skills will always have some level of fear. As I already mentioned falling is a part of tumbling so being unwilling to attempt a skill because you are afraid you MIGHT fall is unrealistic. Some athletes are such perfectionists that it limits them from going for new skills. If one little thing feels off about the pass they will stop mid pass which is never safe nor is it a good habit to train. Although falling isn't failing, it is still ok because we learn from our mistakes. If the athlete never gives themselves the chance to fail they are never giving themselves that chance to learn. Going for a new skill will always push kids out of their comfort zone.

Rushing Through Skills- Athletes who rush through skills without perfecting them or athletes who don't follow tumbling progressions at all will always deal with inconsistency in their tumbling. Basics are there to be the foundation for your tumbling skills. If you don't have a strong foundation you will see athletes regress in their tumbling at some point in their career. We train our athletes to master skills before moving. That's why we have the evaluations at the end of each month in our classes to make sure that skills are not just being thrown but also done correctly. Mastering skills might seem like the athlete is progressing slow but we would rather them progress correctly rather than
fast.

Bad Habits- When a new athlete comes into Justice one of the first things our coaches have to do is break bad habits. In tumbling uncorrected little issues can become big issues in a athlete's long term tumbling career. Sometimes the thing holding a athlete back from gaining a skill is in their basic skills but they don't want to take the time to go back and work on something they already have. We make sure to communicate to the parents and athlete why we are going back and fixing a bad habit.

Outside Stressors- Since there is such a big mental aspect to tumbling there are multiple outside stressors that could lead to mental blocks. Athletes dealing with issues at school or home can find that stress affecting their ability to perform at the level they normally would. Some kids let those bad tumbling days turn into mental blocks. Sometimes it can be tumbling in front of a certain parent throws the athletes tumbling off and that turns into some sort of block. In that case its best that the parents wait in the car or our lobby so your athlete gets the most out of their lessons. Justice Tumbling Company is a judgement free zone where athletes can come focus bettering themselves.

OUTRO

At Justice Tumbling Company we understand every athlete is different and learns at their own pace and in their own way. We make sure that our staff is teaching and spotting consistently throughout the program so your athlete has great experience with whatever coach they are working with. We are so intentional about our training because we know all these things that can lead into athletes developing mental blocks. Any athlete dealing with a mental block in our program must first understand that what they are going through is normal and can be corrected. They must look at their block as a challenge and not a problem. If it's a certain skill that the athlete is blocking on it may be best to take a break from working that skill and try some other skills. Our jobs as couches is to find out what triggers that block and then work on eliminating that trigger. If the athlete is taking the training, doing the drills, doing the homework and conditioning their tumbling will eventually click. We do realistic training at Justice Tumbling Company. Meaning even with all the training in the world the first time the athlete does a skill they are blocking on there will be some sort of pressure. We will push our athletes to get out of their comfort zone and into a learning zone.

"It's part of life to have obstacles. It's about overcoming obstacles; that's the key to happiness.

— Herbie Hancock
Musician

"GREAT ENVIRONMENT FOR KIDS WHO WANT TO LEARN TO TUMBLE! BEST TUMBLING GYM IN TULSA! BEEN GOING THERE SINCE MAY AND HAVE ALREADY LEARNED NEW SKILLS AND TECHNIQUES! RUSTY IS AWESOME!"

— **MICHELLE GUMMERE**

"GREAT TEACHING AND LEARNING ENVIRONMENT. HELPS YOU WITH ANY TUMBLING SKILL YOU ARE WORKING ON. AMAZING COACHES, WHO MAKE SURE TO MAKE YOU FEEL SAFE WHEN GETTING SPOTTED, AND THEY HAVE GREAT COMMUNICATION."

— **BREANA LITTLE**

Tiny Tumbling

Hello again Parents, and welcome to Tiny Tumbling! We are so excited to see your little one take their first steps into the world of tumbling with us! As you know, our Tiny Tumbling program is specifically designed for children between the ages three to six years old. This insures that they're properly introduced to the basics of balance, hand-eye coordination, and body control. Of course safety is always our top priority at Justice Tumbling Co., but we also maintain a fun learning environment that is consistent, yet personal to each child's needs.

Tiny Tumblers will focus on the very basics of tumbling and may even be asked to move up to beginner if we see that they're progressing quickly with their skills and maturity level.

Tiny Tumbling Skills:

- Forward Roll
- Backward Roll
- Lunge/Lever
- Handstands
- Bridges
- Cartwheels
- Back Bend/Bridge Kickover
- Front Limber

MONTH ONE

1. **Goals**

    a. **Balance/Arm Placement:** Athletes will learn how to walk forward and backward on a balance beam to gain balance. Athletes will also learn to keep arms by their ears in everything they do.

    b. **Lunge/Lever:** Athletes will learn the proper body shape for their lunge that they will use for everything in tumbling. This is also where the athlete learns what their dominant tumbling side is (having left leg or right leg in front in lunge). Athletes will also learn what a lever is, which is used in every handstand, cartwheel, and round off. (ILLUSTRATION)

    c. **Forward Roll:** Athletes will learn the correct technique for forward rolls. Start with arms by ears, bend knees while tucking chin to chest. Butt will come over head with hollowed out back causing the forward roll. Roll to feet with arms by ears. (DON'T USE HANDS TO STAND UP!)

2. **Tip From The Coach**

Mastering arm placement at a young age is crucial to developing strong tumbling. Coaches are always having to remind kids of every level to keep arms up and by their ears, but if an athlete masters that at a young age it becomes a good habit they develop.

3. **Practice At Home**

    a. Proper technique forward rolls on a mattress or trampoline.

    b. Lunge reach to lever against a wall.

    c. Arms by ears hop off toes going forward and backward.

> "There are no shortcuts to building a team each season. You build the foundation brick by brick."
> — Bill Belichick
> 8 - Time Superbowl Winning Coach

MONTH TWO

1. Goals

    a. **Backward Roll:** Athletes will learn to do a backward roll down a wedge mat using proper technique. Athletes will start standing with arms by ears and then bend their knees touching their butt to the ground while keeping arms up. As athlete touches butt to the ground they will drive their knees, shins, and toes over their head with their chin tucked to chest. Athletes should finish the backward roll on their feet with arms by their ears. Add using pizza hands to push off ground to stand.

    b. **Bridges:** Athletes will begin to stretch and shape their bodies so they can hold themselves up in a proper technique bridge. Athletes should be able to fall to a bridge from a standing position with arms never leaving ears. Athletes should be able to hold the proper bridge for thirty to sixty seconds.

    c. **Back Bend/Bridge Kickover:** Using mats, athletes will learn to kickover from their bridge preparing them for Back Walkovers. The kickover should finish in a lunge with arms by ears. The goal is to have the athlete start from a standing position with arms by ears on a flat surface, reach to and catch bridge with arms never bending or leaving ears. Then kickover with straight legs finishing in a lunge with arms by ears.

2. Tip From The Coach

STRETCHING IS IMPORTANT. At Justice we stretch before every class, private, and clinic. Anytime an athlete is going to tumble they should stretch before. Having strong tumbling requires flexibility. If you are feeling any kind of pain during the bridge and kickovers then that means you should be stretching more!

4. Practice at home

    a. Proper technique backward rolls on a mattress or trampoline.
    b. Stretching out back to gain flexibility for bridges. (ILLUSTRATION)
    c. Practicing kicking over off a higher surface such as a couch or bed.

"The successful warrior is the average man, with lazer-like focus." - Bruce Lee
Legendary martial arts master and actor

38
MONTH THREE

1. **Goals**

    a. **Handstands:** Athletes will learn how to kick up to a handstand against a wall using mats as well as kicking up to a handstand without having to use a wall to balance them. Athletes should start in their lunge with arms by their ears. Reaching long into their handstand passing through a lever squeezing their legs tight at the top of their handstand and finishing back in their long lunge with arms by their ears.

    b. **Front Limber:** A front limber is a handstand fall to a bridge. This prepares athletes for front walkovers.

    c. **Cartwheel:** Cartwheels should start in a lunge with arms by ears, reach long through the lever with both hands facing the same direction. While upside down the athlete should be in a handstand with their legs split landing back in a lunge facing the direction they just came. (NO STAR CARTWHEELS)

2. **Tip From The Coach**

    • Athletes must have their head in on both handstands and cartwheels.

    • Justice classes want all cartwheels landing in a lunge unless specified differently.

    • Landing in a lunge makes it easy for athletes to progress to a round off.

4. **Practice at Home**

    a. Holding a handstand against a wall for one minute to condition shoulders.

    b. Cartwheels and front limbers can both be practiced at home when they have been mastered in class.

> *"It's the little details that are vital. Little things make big things happen."*
> ## - John Wooden
> Iconic Hall of Fame basketball coach who won ten chanpionships over a twelve year span

NOTES

"GREAT GYM!!!! I HAVE LOOKED FOR A GYM FOR MY DAUGHTER FOR SEVERAL YEARS AND FINALLY FOUND A GREAT TUMBLING GYM.
THE COACHES ARE VERY KNOWLEDGEABLE AND HAVE VERY UPBEAT AND POSITIVE ATTITUDES! I PERSONALLY DID GYMNASTICS AND WAS VERY IMPRESSED WITH THERE COACHING TECHNIQUE."

- KRISTA SHERILL

BEGINNER

Beginner Tumbling classes work many of the same skills as the Tiny Tumbling class, the only difference is the ages for beginner tumbling is seven to eighteen. This class is designed to perfect and master all the fundamental skills needed for the rest of your tumbling career. This class introduces drills for back handsprings. You must master all the beginner skills and evaluate out of the class to move to Novice Class.

Beginning Tumbling Skills:

- *Forward/Backward Roll*

- *Bridge/Bridge Kickover*

- *Handstand*

- *Cartwheel*

- *Front Limber*

- *Round Off*

- *Toe Touch*

MONTH ONE

1. **Goals**

    a. **Forward/Backward Rolls:** Both learned on the wedge mat and then moved to a flat surface. Both rolls will start from a standing position with arms by ears. When rolling keep chin to chest. Forward Roll you drive your butt over your head. Backward Roll you will drive knees, shins, and toes over your head. Both skills finish on feet with arms by ears.

    b. **Bridge/Bridge Kickover:** Making sure all athletes can hold a bridge in the proper position with arms by ears, feet and legs together with legs straight. Bridge Kickover will be learned on a elevated surface and then moved to a flat surface.

    c. **Handstand:** Handstand must start in a lunge with arms by ears. When the athlete kicks to handstand feet must be tight together at the top of the handstand and head must be in with arms by ears. Handstand should finish in a lunge with arms by ears unless specified differently. In class there will be variations of handstands such as handstand snap down rebound, handstand forward roll, and handstand punch off toes back to handstand.

2. **Tip From The Coach**

In your class there will be independent drills and stations set up. These drills/stations are set up to help fix, strengthen, or shape your skills. Do the set number of reps of each drill the coach gives and we promise it will benefit your tumbling. Athletes who do not try on drills or skip drills/stations completely always learn at a slower pace.

4. **Practice at Home**

a. Handstand hold against a wall or having someone assist by holding feet/ankles. Should be able to hold handstand for one minute without struggling.

b. Bridge holds for one minute.

c. Bridge kickovers in class.

d. Forward and backward rolls can be mastered in class.

> "The measure of who we are is how we react to something that doesn't go our way."
> - Gregg Popovich
> 5 - Time NBA champion basketball coach

MONTH TWO

1. **Goals**

    a. **Front Limber:** A front limber is where you kick to handstand and fall to bridge with straight arms. This will prepare athletes for front walkovers. These can be done up on to a wedge mat until athlete is comfortable and then move front limber to a flat surface.

    b. **Cartwheel:** Cartwheels should always start in the long lunge with arms by ears. As the athlete kicks into the cartwheel they should reach their arms out long through a lever with both hands facing the side wall with head in and arms by ears. Cartwheels should finish in a lunge with arms by ears unless specified differently by the coach.

    c. **Roundoff:** Standing roundoffs are a lot like a cartwheel but you snap your feet together at the top as your hands are on the ground. Roundoff should be taught from a standing position then moved to a power hurdle and then two step. Athletes should always finish the round off with arms by ears and chest and head up.

2. **Tip From The Coach**

    • The hurdle before the roundoff should have arms by ears and stretch through a long lunge and lever.

    • All roundoffs should be long, fast, and tight.

4. **Practice At Home**

    a. Practice all types for the roundoff in yard on flat surface. (Standing, Power Hurdler, Two Step)

    b. Only practice cartwheels and roundoffs at home if they are done with the technique taught to you in a Justice Tumbling class.

> "When an athlete has a growth spurt their skills MUST grow with them."
>
> **- Rusty Bratzler**
> Founder of Justice Tumbling Company

MONTH THREE

1. **Goals**

    a. Have Handstand, Cartwheel, Bridge kickover, Front Limber, and Roundoff mastered.

    b. **Starting drills for standing BHS:** Sit jump to elevated mat landing flat on back with arms by ears.

    c. **Starting drills for running round off back handspring:** Long round off over a mat to get spacing correct. Then round off rebound to elevated mats landing flat on back with arms by ears.

2. **Tip From The Coach**

Make sure all drills for Back Handspring are done correctly and only how the coach explains it. When done correctly the drills will develop good habits that make learning a back handspring safe and easy.

4. **Practice At Home**

    a. Holding handstand against the wall for one minute without struggling.

    b. Two Step round off rebound making sure arms never leave ears all the way from the hurdle to the rebound.

    c. Sit jump drills. Start in standing position with head forward, arms by side, and feet together. Bend knees like sitting in a chair with arms swinging back NOT forward. Jump from that position pushing off toes while swinging arms to ears. Control power landing with feet together and arms by ears. HEAD NEVER GOES BACK!

> "If you can not hold a handstand against a wall for a minute you are asking a lot of your body to catch your weight in a back handspring." - Rusty Bratzler
> Founder of Justice Tumbling Company

NOTES

"WE LOVE JUSTICE TUMBLING! THE COACHES ARE AMAZING! THIS IS THE FIRST GYM I HAVE FOUND WHERE THE COACH WILL FIND EACH PARENT AFTER CLASS TO GO OVER HOW THEIR CHILD IS PROGRESSING AND WHAT THEY COULD BE DOING AT HOME PRIOR TO THE NEXT VISIT. IT IS SO NICE AS A PARENT TO GET THOSE UPDATES/RECOMMENDATIONS! COMMUNICATION IS KEY AND THEY HAVE NAILED IT!"

- MEAGHAN GIPSON

Novice

Novice Tumbling class is where athletes get to learn everything there is to know about back handsprings. Athletes will also learn front and back walkovers in this class. To be in this class you must have all your Beginning Tumbling skills mastered. Back handspring is one of the most important skills in tumbling because you will use a back handspring in almost every pass you do for tumbling. Too often we get athletes who have started working back handspring already whether at another gym or on their own on a trampoline, and because of this we end up trying to fix bad habits more so than developing the skill. If an athlete went through and evaluated out of our Beginning Tumbling class it should be a smooth transition into the Novice Tumbling class.

Novice Tumbling Skills:

- *Front Walkover*
- *Back Walkover*
- *Standing Back Handspring*
- *Running Back Handspring*
- *Standing and Running Series*
- *Toe Touch Back Hand Spring*

MONTH ONE

1. **Goals**

    a. **Front Walkover:** Two step hurdle through a long lunge and lever reaching hands long like a handstand blocking through your shoulders the same time you are driving the heel of your front foot over your head. Your legs will stay split as your go over landing in a lunge with arms by ears.

    b. **Back Walkover:** Starting in a lunge with arms by ears the athlete will reach back to a bridge while raising one foot/leg off the ground. As hands touch the ground with arms by ears the athlete will push off the toe still on the ground causing them to be able to get both legs over their head landing in a lunge with arms by ears.

    c. Coaches will take the time to make sure the athletes understand the technique and body shape of back handsprings before allowing athletes to start working on the actual skill. If the athletes have a strong understanding of the skill they are less likely to develop a fear of the skill. There will be a lot of drills and stations for back handsprings set up during class to help shape and strengthen the skill. These should be drills and stations the athlete can perform safely on their own.

2. **Tip From The Coach**

    • Learning a proper technique Back Walkover before a Back Handspring will build the confidence and the technique needed for a Back Handspring.
    • We have our Novice athletes learn front walkover that way when they get their back handspring the athlete should be able to do two step front walkover roundoff back handspring.
    • Don't use your trampoline at home to attempt your back handspring for the first time. This almost always causes bad habits and bad technique that end up hindering the learning process.

4. **Practice at Home**

    a. Start from standing position with arms by ears and reach to bridge without arms bending or ever leaving ears.

    b. Wall sit with heels under knees and legs at ninety-degree angle. This is the same position the athlete should be sitting in for a standing back handspring. The stronger the wall sit the stronger the back handspring.

MONTH TWO

1. **Goals**

    a. By month two novice athletes should have their front and back walkovers.

    b. Drills for standing a running back handspring. Multiple drills and stations will be set up to fix, strengthen, or shape the athletes back handspring during class.

    c. Athletes will start to get a lot of reps in of standing back handspring with a spot from a coach.

2. **Tip From The Coach**

    • Going backwards in a back handspring is usually where kids start to develop fear. That's why our coaches take the time to make sure they explain the technique and do a lot of drills before just being spotted on a back handspring.

    • If you can do a strong standing back handspring by yourself running should be easier, especially with a good roundoff.

    • At this point all athletes should be able to hold a handstand for one minute without struggling.

4. **Practice at Home**

    a. Front walkovers and back walkovers should be practiced at home if they have been mastered in class.

    b. Two step roundoff rebounds done correctly should be practiced at home. Always practicing landing feet together with chest up and arms by ears

> "Each of us must confront our own fears, must come face to face with them. How we handle our fears will determine where we go with the rest of our lives. To experience adventure or to be limited by
>
> **- Judy Blume**
> American Author

MONTH THREE

1. **Goals**

    a. All athletes throwing standing back handspring by themselves on some sort of surface.

    b. Athletes getting a lot of reps in on running tumbling with coaches assistance

    c. Starting drills for Tucks.

    d. The goal at the end of month three is to have all athletes evaluate out of the Novice class and into the Intermediate class.

2. **Tip From The Coach**

    • Even after an athlete masters their backhand spring and round off they should always train them to make sure no bad habits are developed.

4. **Practice at Home**

    a. If you have mastered standing back handspring in class you should be practicing at home on a flat surface or on a trampoline. Don't let tumbling on the trampoline change your technique.

    b. Calf raises to prepare athletes for rebounding into flipping skills.

    c. Plank holds to build up core muscles for flipping skills.

> "Why was 1 the best? What was my secret? 1 never got bored with the basics."
>
> - Kobe Bryant
> 5x NBA Champion

NOTES

"LOVE GOING TO JUSTICE TUMBLING. GREAT COACHES AND ATMOSPHERE!!! WE DRIVE 1 1/2 HOURS TO GO THERE. HIGHLY RECOMMEND IT!!!"

— **DENISE KEATTS**

"RUSTY IS THE TUMBLING COACH FOR MY DAUGHTER'S HIGH SCHOOL TEAM, AND SHE TAKES A CLASS AT JUSTICE. THE SIGN-UP PROCESS WAS SIMPLE, AND SHE LOVES HER CLASSES. RUSTY &
THE REST OF THE STAFF ARE FANTASTIC!"

— **MISTY SMITH**

INTERMEDIATE

Intermediate Class is where you begin to flip with no hands going forward and backward. If the athlete followed the progressions of the Beginner and Novice then the athlete should already have strong fundamentals, basics, and back handsprings. Flipping without hands requires a lot of technique and mental toughness on the athletes part. If the athlete does not have strong Beginner and Novice skills it can prolong learning the intermediate skills. The athlete should have all the Intermediate skills mastered before moving onto Advanced skills.

Intermediate Tumbling Skills:

Running Tumbling

- *Punch Front*
- *Roundoff Back Handspring Tuck*
- *Roundoff Tuck*
- *Roundoff Series to Tuck*

Standing Tumbling

- *Standing Tuck*
- *Series to Tuck*

MONTH ONE

1. **Goals:**

    a. The goals in the first month with Intermediate skills is for the athletes to understand the technique required for each skill and to have perfected the drills for each skill. It is important for the athlete to remember that the tuck should happen in three parts. I)The Lift 2)The Flip 3)The Landing. Also, There could be the added step of using arms to grab. Using the arms to grab should only happen after the rotation for the flip has started. The arms grabbing for the knees should be an afterthought.

    b. Standing series going up a wedge mat

    c. Punch Front setting drills

    d. Have athletes doing drills for standing tucks

2. **Tip From The Coach**

    • The more knowledge you have of a skill the less scary that skill will be. That's why our coaches take the time to explain the technique and set up drills.

    • Being quick to punch off your toes will help lift your flipping skills.

3. **Practice at Home**

    a. Standing series to rebound making sure legs and feet stay together and arms stay by ears.

    b. Sit ups without shoulders touching the ground that way the athletes core is engaged the whole time. (3 sets of 10)

    c. Laying on back with hands under something to weigh down. Athletes will raise toes then hips to ceiling into a candlestick position and then lower themselves down never letting heels touch the ground.

"The hard work definitely paid off and hard work always does."

- Gabby Douglas
Olympic Gold Winning Gymnast

MONTH TWO

1. **Goals**

    a. In the second month of Intermediate we want all athletes throwing punch front by themselves.

    b. Have a station dedicated to roundoff multiple back handsprings to rebound to prepare for series to tuck.

    c. Athletes getting a lot of reps in on running tucks with coaches assistance.

    d. Have athletes landing standing tuck on their own off elevated surface, spring board, or air floor.

2. **Tip From The Coach**

    • Don't practice flipping skills on trampoline at home until flipping skills are mastered in class.

    • When setting for a tuck, athlete should be in a controlled straight line from toes to fingertips while arms are by ears as the toes leave the floor.

3. **Practice at Home**

    a. Athletes should be doing some sort of core exercise every other day.
    - Leg Lifts: 3x10
    - Toe Touches: 3x20
    - Planks: 1 min 2x

    b. Athletes should be doing calf raises to strengthen rebounds for tucks and to strengthen ankles in case the athlete lands short on a tuck.

    c. ABC's to strengthen ankles.

"You can't win unless you learn how to lose."

- Kareem Abdul-Jabbar
6x NBA Champion

MONTH THREE

1. **Goals**

    a. In the third month of Intermediate class we want all athletes to be throwing a running tuck by themselves whether it's a roundoff tuck or a back handspring tuck.

    b. Continue strengthening running and standing series.

    c. Have athletes landing standing tucks on spring or hard floor.

    d. Start doing drills for Layouts.

2. **Tip From The Coach**

    • If the back handsprings are high the tuck will be low. Long back handsprings equal high tucks.

    • The tighter the tuck the faster the rotation.

3. **Practice at Home**

    a. Hollow body holds to get the body ready for layouts (give time)
    (ex: 30/3x or 1 min/3x daily)

    b. At this point the athlete should be conditioning ankles daily with calf raises. (See month 2 for detailed workout)

"Sports have become increasingly more specialized, but that doesn't mean they shouldn't be fun."

- Mia Hamm
Olympic Gold Winning Soccer Player

NOTES

"JUSTICE TUMBLING HAS BEEN A WONDERFUL EXPERIENCE FOR US! RUSTY IS AMAZING WITH THESE KIDS! IT IS CLEAR THAT HIS COMPASSION & KNOWLEDGE OF TUMBLING ALLOWS HIM TO TAP
INTO THE WAY EACH INDIVIDUAL CHILD WORKS & PERSONALIZE THEIR TIME WITH HIM. WE LOVE THE WAY HE FOCUSES ON THE DETAILS OF HOW & WHY SOMETHING IS OR ISN'T WORKING TO HELP YOU MOVE FORWARD WITH YOUR TUMBLING."

- PATTY JONES, PARENT

ADVANCED

Advanced class is where athletes will be working on more difficult flipping skills. In running tumbling athletes will be focusing on layouts and more difficult specialty passes. In standing tumbling athletes will focus on adding skill to their standing tuck as well as standing series to layout. All advanced skills require a lot of technique, body control, and power to be done safely. There will be drills set up in advanced class that help the athlete with all three.

Advanced Skills:

Running Tumbling

- *Layout*
- *Whip*
- *Punch Front Step Off*
- *Specialty to Layout*

Standing Tumbling

- *Toe Touch Back*
- *Cartwheel Back*
- *Back Handspring Back*
- *Series to Layout*

MONTH ONE

1. **Goals**

    a. Coaches should take time to explain in detail the technique required for each advanced skill that way the athlete understands what is expected of them when either doing the actual skill or doing a drill for that skill.

    b. Athletes learn the drills required for each of the advanced skills.

    c. By the end of month one athletes should be able to do advanced drills independently that way the coach can be spotting athletes on their advanced skills.

2. **Tip From The Coach**

    • Most athletes don't want to take the time to master a layout and want to move onto doing a full. The stronger the layout the easier it is to learn a full.

    • Doing advanced drills confidently on their own will help athletes develop the mental strength to go for the actual skill on their own.

3. **Practice at Home**

    a. Hollow body holds for conditioning layout position. Hollow body rocks 3x10 - 20

    b. Candlestick Holds (3x10 - 20)

> "In Tulsa, it was sports or nothing."
>
> **- Bill Hader**
> Actor, Comedian, Writer, and Producer

MONTH TWO

Goals

a. Athletes are able to do drills on their own while getting a lot of reps in on running tumbling with the assistance of a coach.

b. Athletes doing drills for specialty passes on their own.

Tip From The Coach

• Layouts set high while whips stretch long. Make sure your layout technique is nothing like your whip technique.

Practice at Home

a. Still conditioning candlestick holds and hollow body holds. (See month 1 for #'s)

b. Sticking standing tucks with feet together.

"You can look for external sources of motivation and that can catalyze a change, but it won't sustain one. It has to be from an internal desire."
- Jillian Michaels
Fitness Trainer, Business Woman, Author

MONTH THREE

1. **Goals**

    a. By the end of month three the goal is to have every athlete doing all advanced skills on their own so they can move into the elite class.

    b. Starting drills for spinning.

2. **Tip From The Coach**

    • Train yourself to be a well-rounded tumbler. Don't limit yourself to one specialty skill. Be able to do multiple specialty skills that way you can add all your skills into one elite pass.

    • Whatever issues an athlete is having on a layout technique they are more than likely going to have the same technique issues in their full.

3. **Practice at Home**

    a. Hollow body roll to stomach and then roll back to hollow body

    b. ANY AND ALL CORE EXERCISES!!!

"The key to success is to focus our conscious mind on things we desire not things we fear."

- Brian Tracy
Motivational Speaker

NOTES

"I HAVE BEEN TUMBLING WITH RUSTY FOR ALMOST 4 YEARS. I LOVE THE ENVIRONMENT THERE AS SOON AS I WALK IN I AM WELCOMED BY RUSTY'S WIFE CAITLIN OR HIS MOM. I LOVE BEING THERE BECAUSE I AM INSPIRED TO GET NEW SKILLS. RUSTY ALWAYS MAKES SURE THAT EVERYONE HAS A SMILE ON THERE FACE AND THAT EVERYONE IS HAPPY AND HAVING A GOOD TIME. I LOVE TUMBLING THERE!"

- KYNLEE ACKLIN

ELITE

Advanced class is where athletes will be working on more difficult flipping skills. In running tumbling athletes will be focusing on layouts and more difficult specialty passes. In standing tumbling athletes will focus on adding skills to their standing tuck as well as standing series to layout. All advanced skills require a lot of technique, body control, and power to be done safely. There will be drills set up in advanced class that help the athlete with all three.

Elite Skills:

- *Front Handspring Up*
- *Cartwheel Up*
- *Back Handspring Up*
- *Hand in Hand*
- *Rewinds*
- *Double Up*

Bases Working:

- *Throwing Stunts with Flips and Inversions*
- *Proper Flick Placement and Positioning*
- *Hand Placement and Absoption*

Flyers Working:

- *Inversions and Flipping into Stunts*
- *Body Positioning and Timing*
- *Placing and Rollling*

MONTH ONE

1. **Goals**

    a. Coaches should take time to explain in detail the technique required for each advanced skill that way the athlete understands what is expected of them when either doing the actual skill or doing a drill for that skill.

    b. Athletes learn the drills required for each of the advanced skills.

    c. By the end of month one athletes should be able to do advanced drills independently that way the coach can be spotting athletes on their advanced skills.

2. **Tip From The Coach**

    • Most athletes don't want to take the time to master a layout and want to move onto doing a full. The stronger the layout the easier it is to learn a full.

    • Doing advanced drills confidently on their own will help athletes develop the mental strength to go for the actual skill on their own.

3. **Practice at Home**

    a. Hollow body holds for conditioning layout position. (2x30)

    b. Candlestick Holds

"I really love training and being in good shape, and it's so much a part of my life now, so it never really feels like work to me."
- Tom Brady
NFL Quarterback

MONTH TWO

1. **Goals**

    a. Athletes getting a lot of reps in on their running elite skills and athletes being able to do elite drills independently.

    b. Athletes should be conditioned enough to do multiple stations of running, standing, and drills for the entire class.

2. **Tip From The Coach**

    • Do not skip stations. The station, whether it be a drill or tumbling station, is set up to condition the athletes technique as well as their endurance. An elite tumbling class should be a work out for the athlete.

    • Trust yourself when doing elite skills. If a Justice coach is allowing you to do the skill by yourself then that means that they believe in you. You have to believe in yourself and your technique.

3. **Practice at Home**

    a. Always conditioning mastered standing and running tumbling skills as much as possible so not to lose any skills

    b. Always conditioning core, knees, and ankles.

"I fear not the man who has practiced 10,000 kicks once, but I fear the man who has practiced one kick 10,000 times."
- Bruce Lee
  Legendary martial arts master and actor

MONTH THREE

1. **Goals**

    a. Athletes should be gaining new skills and passes. The more specialty skills a athlete has mastered the more creative passes they can perform.

    b. Always cleaning up and perfecting all skills.

2. **Tip From The Coach**

    • Trust the Justice method. If you are doing the homework, making the corrections, listening to the podcasts, and trusting your coaches then every athlete no matter how talented can always become a stronger tumbler.

    • Always be picky on your landings in spinning skills. Protect your knees.

3. **Practice at Home**

    a. Always condition mastered skills.

    b. Always condition legs using weights to protect from knee injury.

    c. Always condition core muscles.

"You sort of start thinking anything's possible if you've got enough nerve."

- J.K. Rowling
Author and Creator of Harry Potter

NOTES

"HONESTLY RUSTY IS THE BEST TUMBLING COACH I'VE WORKED WITH IN MY 13 YEARS OF COMPETITIVE CHEERLEADING. HE HELPS YOU UNDERSTAND THE PHYSICAL ASPECT OF TUMBLING BUT BEST OF ALL THE MENTAL WHICH MAKES A WORLD OF DIFFERENCE! HE'S AN AMAZING PERSON AND EASILY THE ONE OF THE BEST COACHES IN THE INDUSTRY WITHOUT FAIL.."

— REAGAN BUSH

STUNTING

At Justice Tumbling Company our main focus is tumbling, but we offer everything an athlete would need to make whatever team they are trying out for. We offer stunt classes as well as a stunt open gym. These classes are for bases and flyers to work on new skills and master old skills. The stunt class is for athletes who want a more one on one with the stunt coaches. Like our tumbling classes, the stunt class and open gym both follow progressions created by the Justice staff. Unlike our tumbling classes the stunt class follows a five to one coach to athlete ratio so the athletes get a ton of work with the coaches. You must enroll in one of the memberships for the stunt class. The stunt open gym has a walk in fee and is open to anyone. On the following pages are a list of group and coed stunt progressions color coded by level as well as what the bases and flyer will work on in each level. Before being put into a class the athlete will do an evaluation with the stunt coach to make the correct class placement.

COED STUNT CLASS LEVELS / SKILLS

BEGINNER

Skills
- ☐ Toss Drill
- ☐ Toss Hands
- ☐ Walk up to Hands
- ☐ Toss Hands Extension

Bases Working
- ☐ How and when to throw
- ☐ Timing of toss and proper technique using leg power and control
- ☐ Flicking through the top and absorbing with legs
- ☐ Hand placement on feet
- ☐ Bump-adjusts
- ☐ Correct Pop-off

Flyers Working
- ☐ Proper jump and flick technique and timing
- ☐ Body positioning in the air
- ☐ Correct pop-off

NOVICE

Skills
- ☐ Bump and go extension
- ☐ Hands lib, stretch, arabesque, scorpion, Y-scale
- ☐ Bump and go lib, stretch, arabesque, scorpion, Y-scale

Bases Working
- ☐ Flicking through the top and using legs to dip under the stunt to hit at the top
- ☐ Pushing stunts to extension level

Flyers Working
- ☐ Continuation of proper flick and feet placement in the air
- ☐ Riding momentum to pull stunts to extension

INTERMEDIATE

Skills
- ☐ Toss target
- ☐ Hands awesome (cupie)
- ☐ Toss lib, stretch, awesome (cupie)
- ☐ Toss low to high lib/stretch

Bases Working
- ☐ Tossing to the top to immediate stunts
- ☐ Proper stunt hand placement and leg absorption

Flyers Working
- ☐ Pulling immediate stunts tossing to the top
- ☐ Focus on staying in tube
- ☐ Foot placement on switches and ball-ups

ADVANCED

Skills
- ☐ Walk up low to high
- ☐ Full up
- ☐ Ball up lib/stretch
- ☐ Full around
- ☐ High to high

Bases Working
- ☐ Adding variations of stunts
- ☐ Flick initiation
- ☐ Spins and re-catching

Flyers Working
- ☐ Flick initiation
- ☐ Spinning in tube
- ☐ Proper feet placing

ELITE

Skills
- ☐ Front handspring up
- ☐ Cartwheel up
- ☐ Back handspring up
- ☐ Hand in Hand
- ☐ Rewinds
- ☐ Double up

Bases Working
- ☐ Throwing stunts with flips and inversions
- ☐ Proper flick placement and positioning
- ☐ Hand placement and absorption

Flyers Working
- ☐ Inversions and flipping into stunts
- ☐ Body positioning and timing
- ☐ Placing and rolling

HOW MANY CAN YOU CHECK OFF?

"HONESTLY RUSTY IS THE BEST TUMBLING COACH I'VE WORKED WITH IN MY 13 YEARS OF COMPETITIVE CHEERLEADING. HE HELPS YOU UNDERSTAND THE PHYSICAL ASPECT OF TUMBLING BUT BEST OF ALL THE MENTAL WHICH MAKES A WORLD OF DIFFERENCE! HE'S AN AMAZING PERSON AND EASILY THE ONE OF THE BEST COACHES IN THE INDUSTRY WITHOUT FAIL."

- AUSTIN ROBLES

www.ingramcontent.com/pod-product-compliance
Lightning Source LLC
Chambersburg PA
CBHW080023110526
44587CB00021BA/3746